The Eighth Color of a Rainbow

Inspirational Poems

Teens * Youth *Adults

The Eighth Color of a Rainbow

Inspirational Poems

Teens * Youth *Adults

Aananya

ZORBA BOOKS

Published in India by Zorba Books, 2019

Website: www.zorbabooks.com
Email: info@zorbabooks.com

Copyright © **Aananya**

ISBN : 978-93-88497-62-6
eBook ISBN: 978-93-88497-63-3

Zorba Books Pvt. Ltd.(opc)
Gurgaon, INDIA

For The Unheard Voices

ACKNOWLEDGEMENTS

The fact remains that this book would not have come about if it was not for some special people.

My teachers, Mrs. Kavita Harsana, for reading my work, making me believe in myself and helping me to grow. Thank you, ma'am, for distorting my reality field.

Mrs. Sapna Bakshi for always encouraging me to get my words out on paper. "If it were not for you, I would not have words to call my own. Thank you, ma'am."

Mrs. Ananya Nag, "ma'am you gave my deepest and quietest thoughts, shape. Talking to you gave my sentiments a form. Thank you, ma'am."

I wish to thank my principal Mrs. Rupa Chakravarty, for her unstinted support, for always being with me in whatever I did. "Thank you very much, ma'am."

I thank my publishers for always bearing with me, being so supportive and hardworking and the astounding team at Zorba. Thank you for bringing life to this book.

A special thanks to my father, who believes that no matter where I go and what I do, I can succeed. Thank you, dad, for supporting me, always having your back and constantly pushing me forward

Thank you, mom, for being my source of energy and helping me to keep going.

Lastly, a big thank you to my friends!

Thank you, Aris, for reading my poems as soon as I wrote them and for giving me an honest opinion.

Thank you Abhimanyu and Navya for bearing with my elated state every time I wrote something new, re-reading my drafts and telling me that I can achieve something.

My sincere gratitude to all of you, if it were not for you, I would be just another unheard voice. Thank you.

FOREWORD

There are some moments in life that bring us unadulterated joy.

We wish for bliss to stay and so we try to record those moments.

Journals, photographs, stories, they are our ways of capturing the moments we treasure.

If we don't record them, we tend to forget what it was that gave us that sublime happiness, as for the times that led our eyes to water, they stay with us even when we don't want them to.

Happiness is a mood.

Darkness is a phase.

Happiness is fleeting, transient. It comes and leaves just as fast.

Dark times sear themselves into us.

Tear streams lined with thorns etch a bloody trail on our soul.

The fleeting moments of bliss can stay though. We need to hold on.

Happiness is a choice and it's up to us to make it.

Time goes by, it passes as we wish for it to.

We alone hold the ability to make our smiles stay.

We pull life's strings. since long foretold.

Some moments are such; they wash our face with a smile.

And at that moment, more than anything we want time to stop.

CONTENTS

ORIGINALITY

KEEP GOING

BROKEN WORLD

UNSEEN SOMETHINGS

UNSPOKEN SOMETHINGS

LIVING LIFE AS IT GOES

ORIGINALITY

The Eighth Color Of A Rainbow

Melancholy comes from within,
When you know you're differently wired
But no one appreciates it
You know it is a gift
Yet the ignorance;
You can't take it.
Everyone lives under the clouds,
I live above them;
So different I am from humans
That I relate more with aliens.
A change,
You are here to bring it
But the world won't accept it.
So what to do?
Cry and cringe?
In their noggin you are a catastrophe
But in my vision of precision,
There is more to see.
Become what they see
With robotic eyes;
That helps them view the awkward
As unique and wise.

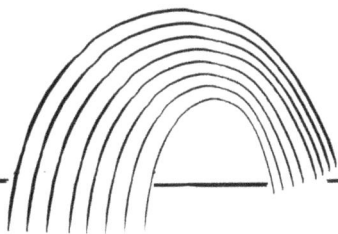

Aananya

Right now they see you
As the eighth misfit in a rainbow
But oh how you enhance its beauty,
They will soon know.

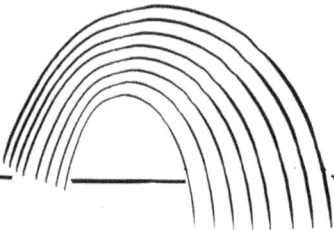

Original

You ever wonder why
Your perspective is different?
You ever realize how
You never mix in the crowd?
There is a reason.
You are special,
You are unique
You are you.
Don't waste it trying to be someone
You know you are not.
Originality is rare,
From you it will begin;
Do stop trying so hard to fit in.
People might not like you,
You might be stranded in the fake eternity
But at least
You will have your dignity.
I might not be the "cool kind"
I may not have colored hair
But what is beneath this mop of back
Is limited edition and works fairly well.
I don't remind anyone
Of anyone.

Aananya

The reason why,
Is not a long story;
The truth is
I am my only copy.
When I grow up
I don't want to be him or her
Not the next Tai Tzu ying
Nor the other Shakespeare.
I want to earn recognition,
Before the oblivion occurs
I want to be successful
Ere we burn under the sun
I want to be known as "she was the only one".

©

Iceberg

To judge and to offend
They are different yet related somehow
You do the former
And the latter will tag along
When you see something
You can't unsee it
When you hurt someone
Neither can you heal the wound
Nor can you undo it
To judge and to offend
They are different yet related somehow
You were insensitive back then
What makes you sorry now?
Small minds hold grudges
Great ones forgive
I am not narrow-minded
So forgiveness you might as well expect
But what you did and said
I will never forget
It is good what you did
In an explicable way it really is
I sing with all my soul

Aananya

I sing all night long
When I get tired I remember how you shunned my song
That alone gives me the cojones to get up
Go on and prove you wrong
An iceberg I am at frozen sea
Your words are ice and they build me
I appear small
And you give your judgement
What you never realize is
That I use the ice you throw at me
To build my foundation
There is more to me
Than what meets the eye
Small I might appear
Nevertheless there is more to see 'neat the surface
I am not crystal clear
So judge me all you want
It only helps
When the sunrise strikes me
You admire me
Even though it is out of sheer envy
However, when you hit me
Try to break my solid build
Is when you see how brazen I am
And invite trouble your way
An Iceberg I am
An iceberg I'll stay.

KEEP GOING

The Second Time

It is an interesting life,
Till a certain point,
Every opportunity comes twice.
If you fail once, don't you cry,
You will get one more chance to rejoice.
People will tease,
The masses will mock,
In your brain, they will try to wreak havoc.
Don't fall in a trance,
Don't lose your calm;
Remember you have got one more chance.
Let people say what they please,
Meanwhile prepare for your victory.
A third chance won't come across,
So when the second comes,
Like lichen you must grasp.
Forget your past all right,
The only memory should be,
Which wrong you need to right.
Life is interesting yet uncertain somehow,
It gives a second chance then or now.

Aananya

Use it right or be oppressed under life's might.
Sooner or later your day will arrive,
That day you must shine bright,
Prove every person wrong who thought he was right.

Iron Lady

The world is a harsh place
You need to help yourself
Pleasant with a hint of toughness
Manoeuvre your life
Like a sorceress
Calm and collected
Keep your composure
It is you against the whole world
But you are never over.
Wait fore you let the vexation vent
Refrain from getting tense
Your only hamartia
Should be your strength
All you can do
Is give your best
Give it all that you have
And karma will see to the rest
Do not permit nerves
To get the better of you
That is the last thing you want
As it makes the uphill battle moot
End of the day,

Aananya

The sorceress is you
Do not let anything hinder your way
Do what you what you have to.
Cry a river
Build a bridge
Wear a smile
And get over it.
Look your enemy in the eye
See the hatred
Turn into envy
That is when you know
You've come a long way iron lady.

Recovery

Your words leave an impact,
Deeper than you believe.
Your statements can change lives.
Can heal a broken part,
Or break a healing heart.
There is dusk before dawn,
Every fight you will win
Provided you use brain over brawn.
People get angry,
They get riled;
Tangled in panic,
Often lose their mind.
Under the mistletoe
Sitting on their hinds
Over their loss they will whine.
You become what you put your mind to
When you fall,
Get up and stand twice as tall.
Don't spiral down or cry on your loss
With a mind that distorts all,
But the birds eye;
Head up to bring order from chaos.

Aananya

It is hard for him to relapse
He who doesn't commit the same mistake twice
As for he who does,
The spotlight was never his to shine.

Fear No More

In the quietest corners
Reside the loudest hearts
The most tortured souls
Bloom to be the strongest
Suppress them with all your power
They ricochet twice as hard
They never truly fail
As they never really stop
Hate them
Or not
It will not influence them
Their strength lies within
Far from mortal reach
You cannot demolish them.
They are lotuses
They burgeon from the dirt
They are warriors
They fight until they prevail
Left behind
The entirety of trepidation
Risen above all the voices
That ever pulled them down.

Aananya

These clouds hold
Your downbeat thoughts
They rain down just when
You think they've lost.

BROKEN WORLD

Wrinkled Jeans

The horizon is speckled,
Not with stars but with building lights.
Drifting around corners,
The car felt airtight,
Glancing out of the window,
I stared into the starless starry night.
In this pretentious world,
Nothing feels realistic;
The fauna is endangered,
And the flora is plastic.
Such a drastic turn events have taken
We made hell of what once was Eden.
In this suffocating atmosphere,
Fresh air isn't ample,
Breathing in the chemical laden air,
Is like putting gun to the temple.
Industrialization and chemicals,
For the abode's pollution they blame it;
But the hypocrites do nothing to save it.
The shimmering star,
Is now a gray stone,
To extinction we Homo sapiens are prone.

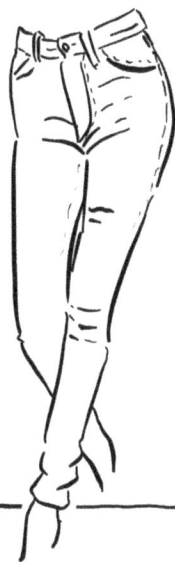

Aananya

The damage we have caused,
Is like a pair of wrinkled and starched jeans;
No matter how much you iron them,
They just won't be straight and clean.

Look Outside To See Inside

Will it rain today?
Will it get sunnier than it already is?
So much goes on in my head
As I look out the window
With milk and bread.
I am not a fun of the sun
The paining light,
Gets everyone riled
Ever ready to fight.
On the contrary
When there is dark during the day
And cool wind lightens your way;
The breeze blows your hair
Lost in deep thought,
For a change you just don't care,
The smell of rain
Adding subtlety to the atmosphere.
Life is an endless chain of boulevards
You wake alone
Occasionally pulled back by ghosts of the past.
The wind catches pace
Getting wilder with time,

Aananya

You try but fail to rewind
Dejection, rejection,
Absence of gratification
A bubble of isolation
Bliss readily invited
To peace's cremation.
So much turbulence in your mind,
The nature is a mirror
For your soul
The winds getting torment
Disruption is crystal clear
Now the rain comes down,
Blending with your tears.
The gaia knows you
Better than you think;
Your state of mind
Before your eyes
Every time you blink.
When you are on the edge of breaking down
And you feel nothing but frowns
Close your eyes and take a break,
Lose yourself in the sun's warm embrace;
When you are true to yourself
No problem is too big to face.
As I look out of the window
So much goes on in my head

The Eighth Color of a Rainbow

As I finish the milk
And choke down the bread.
The environment knows me
Better than I know myself.
This feeling however,
Will not last forever
There will be a time
We will be overcome with terror
And the damaged nature won't be here
To provide cover.

War Left Humanity Afar

There are wars being fought
There is blood in the streets
There is suffering as far as I can see
This was not how it was meant to be.

There are people dying, people dead.
Children are being born amidst violence and bloodshed
There are so many more broken
I look around, and see
That things are not the worst for me.

There are bombs being blasted
Lives are being crafted
In such a way that their
Lights are stolen
And their skies are tinted grey.

The fighting needs to stop
The suffering needs to cease
It kills me to witness
The death of humanity

The Eighth Color of a Rainbow

It didn't have to be this way
But it's the path
We've chosen to go
Where emotions are dead
And feelings are frozen
In the snow.

A Big Bad World

Champions aren't born
Champions are made
Nourished with affection
Toughened with curses
Nurtured with ministration.
With that in constant supply
They only evolve
Never quit before they try
All issues they solve.
You can only travel so far
With people associated
But the journey knows no bounds
If you set out departed.
People are strings
They hold you back,
Cut your wings
Don't let you fly.
Cut these strings ere they cut you;
Block out their worthless word
And in the dreams' sky
A free bird you will soar.
Walk alone

The Eighth Color of a Rainbow

But walk steady;
Ease yourself
But always be ready.
In this superficial world
Good times are long gone
Trust is torn,
Friendships worn.
It is a big bad world
And you are on your own.

UNSEEN SOMETHINGS

An Old Melody

No I can't go back
To what I used to be
I have come a mile too far
The former me has become a memory
A long lost melody
On my deaf ears which
Which falls pointlessly
I speak an uncanny language
Where 'not again'
Translates to 'it's okay'
I hide the feelings that are true
With every breath I swallow my rage
Once was infested
By a dark entity
As it grew I realized
That it has always been me.

The Deceptive Curve

There are only so many smiles
That one can fake
Only so many betrayals that one can take.
The perfect curve
Does so much to hide
Everything that is broken
On the inside.
There for everyone
Always by their side
Yet so often stranded by self
The tears well up
Forming a tide
Only for so long the walls,
Can keep this tide out
The damage is done
There's nothing left to do but shout
Why must we block
Those who care
Their smiles we rob
But their pain we don't share
The majority fails to look beyond
Seeking empty validation
To superficiality they're growing fond.

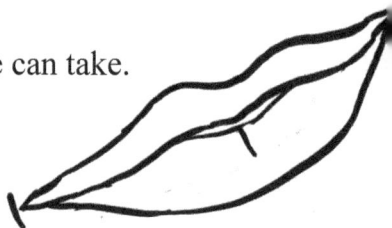

The Eighth Color of a Rainbow

No close ties this way
Will be established
Its funny how connections
Seem to have perished.
A tear almost surfaced
Waved it off and smirked
Was smiled at
The deception has worked.

The Truth Of Lies

The truth will always hurt,
Lies offer nothing
But false sense of comfort.
A painkiller shielding
The wound that exists,
The medicine all are using
But pain still persists.
Covering the cure isn't a solution
Procrastinating war doesn't relieve tension.
Torments the liar and he who was lied to
Igniting a fire,
Washed only by words that are true.
A surgery pains
But that is temporary,
On the fire it rains;
Curing wounds ultimately.
Better a slap
Than a kiss of thorns;
Better the truth
Than lies that are worn.
I'd rather be wounded
Than be scarred;

The Eighth Color of a Rainbow

I choose to lose,
Over playing a torturous game;
As time passes,
Wounds heal
But scars still remain the same.

More Than Just Eyes

So much lies in the eyes of the listener
So much not heard is spoken,
Look beyond the cheerful smile
And see the heart that is broken.
The grief in their eyes
When they claim to be content,
What is truly inside
Is so much different.
From whom they portray themselves to be,
People are never what they seem.
Smiles are covers
That conceals the agony,
The façade they wear
Tells a story
One that makes legend
Out of reality.
Look around and see
Nobody has it all
But everyone portrays it to be
Something else;

The Eighth Color of a Rainbow

Let us not get caught
In the show humans put up
And see them for their real selves.
Once trust is broken
You can never build it to be the same
You can see shattered belief in their pupils
And the hateful world is to blame.
But there's yourself,
You can always trust;
There is hope that you can forever have,
There is the voice in your head
That tells you to continue believing,
Your talent which is the crutch
When your legs stop moving.
The universe loves to troll,
Your happiness and confidence
It might take,
But it can't take your soul

UNSPOKEN SOMETHINGS

The Smallest Voices Make It Major

A Human can only meet its mate
And never know they are meant
For various factors out shadow the heart,
Its voice the smallest
And the aggregate,
Yells the loudest.
And so The Human erases
What destiny thoughtfully marked;
With blood and tears
The Human writes,
What was never meant.
Overcome with melancholia,
Agonizingly accepting,
What was never his.

Solitude

Words don't do justice
To the abstract way I feel
So many aspects that they miss
My life is rolling on a reel.
Never taken seriously
But I can't blame you
Always smiling happily
How will you know that my pain is true?
So why don't I lose this mask
Why do I always conceal
Is it so impossible of a task
To reveal the way I feel
All tears I always waiver
For my apathetic company will only tease
And so I put the pen to paper
This way my suffering I ease
I've become what no one can embrace
Stone cold on the inside
A warm smile on my face
Tired of having an invisible presence

The Eighth Color of a Rainbow

It gets frustrating
To have valueless existence
But I'd rather be with me
Than be lonely
In someone else's company.

Anxiously Beautiful

My hands are salty
From wiping tears
Some are mine
Some another soul's fears.
Your tears cause
My wounds to burn
I have had a fair share of pain
Can you stand through your turn?
In your eyes
I see concealed affliction
I feel your soul yearn
For unattainable perfection.
You get so lost in this quest
To become what does not exist
Losing sense of reality
Agonising delusions persist.
You live a life of what ifs
Losing sense of what is still
Smoke and mirrors embrace your destination
And the real journey you kill.
We all have a hamartia
It helps shape us

The Eighth Color of a Rainbow

a major part of our persona
Not something venomous
It's yours just as much
As your strengths are
A part of you
Not something to be ashamed of
We all have scars
To conceal them you make a law
But what matters is
How beautifully you wear your flaws.

Cursed

How hard can it be?
To not worry?
How hard is it to not make?
Every situation a catastrophe?
Why must we always be,
A selfless being
Whose hurt no one can see?
Why is it that I
Always look at what lies beyond
Those smiling eyes?
But I am human too,
This everyone fails to realize.
I can and I always feel
The ache when you smile,
I know what is real
I know your tears are welling up in a venomous vial.
But why is it that you
So wonderfully fail to see the world
Like I do.
The bathroom tiles
Are my only true friends
For they have seen me
When my concern for this apathetic world ends.

The Eighth Color of a Rainbow

The silent darkness makes me see
The iron harness
Which ties my heart that is a banshee.
My agony I will
Perpetually conceal,
Even though my heart stands still
As my smile bleeds whilst helping you heal.
People say
That I understand this world in a pure way;
They say it is a blessing
However, it only makes my world worse,
Little do they know,
I live life under a curse.

LIVING LIFE AS IT GOES

How Old Are You

Growing up,
As a petite kid;
You would look up to the sky
And wish to work in buildings that scrape it.
When you were little,
You would act all grown
And wish to be on your own;
But it when it comes to your desires
Like the kid you are,
You'd cry and moan.
In your heart a kid;
In your head all grown.
This behaviour is old hat,
Been happening since long
Nothing new;
So really
How old are you?
When you are over twenty three
Got responsibilities,
Finally standing on your own feet
Not very deep inside,
Your heart silently weeps;

Aananya

Wishes to be the kid
It long ago used to be
Are you an old crow
Or a bubbly duckling?
Are you waiting to reap the fruits
Of seeds you'd once sown
Or are you digging in the mud
With excitement
This is a story,
One hundred percent true
Begs the question though;
How old are you?
When you had candy,
You'd save it for later,
When later came,
The sweet had gone bitter.

Let Me Tell You A Story

Happiness is in the way
You look at a situation;
Not in the situation.
The secret is in the revelation,
You either win
Or you learn
You never lose as it is success that you yearn.
A story can be affirmative
Alternatively, negative
It all comes down
To how you narrate it.
When stuck in the gray
Find reasons to be merry;
The answer to why is extremely easy;
Beauty lies in the eyes of the beholder,
You will love the heat
When it gets colder.

Scalar Life

Walking down the boulevard of life,
Everyone runs by
You walk slowly at the edge of a knife
Careful in every step,
Amidst these streets
Your childhood is kept
Had it been buoyant,
You realize it will never be the same.
Had it been a sad one;
You are probably relieved
In the past, it is gone.
So now when you walk
With the shadows,
With only an illusion of bliss
Your sole comfort being,
The Sun's golden kiss;
Thinking about all the opportunities
You did successfully miss,
Lost in your thoughts
Over thinking everything,
In your head, you yourself wreak havoc,
Walking down the road
With only twists and turns

The Eighth Color of a Rainbow

To keep you from reaching
What you badly desire,
In circles the sea churns.
Life goes on with speed,
Not with velocity;
Unfortunate it may sound
But that is the strange reality.
Progress is what all and sundry is showing;
Yet the questions that remain unanswered are;
Where do we come from?
And where are we going?
This journey aint going to be half as pretty,
Unprecedented in every way;
Life is scalar,
A directionless quantity.

Boycotted!

The people I chose to prioritize
The same ones I loved unconditionally
Started feeling distant recently
Apparently, like an option
They chose to leave me
Everything is uglier up close
I happen to be no exception
The closer we get
The sooner you realize
What I sport is just an illusion
To find someone who
Is ready to embrace
Your pretty side
And scarred face
Is extremely rare and beautiful
For it gives purpose to live
The façade you wear is exhaustive
And when it comes off
You will be Boycotted.
People are with you
For momentarily bliss
Along with love and affection that you give
But you can also be rough

The Eighth Color of a Rainbow

The former everyone will love
And buoyantly tolerate
The latter which no one will bear
Boycotted I was
For being myself
My crystal façade
Became broken glass
Shadows of eternal bodies
The only ones that came to sweep
Left with my cracked shell
I picked my pieces
My soul the bouteille
Learned to be content
In my own company
For no one will ever love the raw me.
The silence is deafening
But I've grown to like it.
My gratification,
I can draw;
I am the only one
Who will nourish my flaws.

Sleeping In The Future

When the going gets tough
And the tough can't get going,
When today gets too rough
And you are sick of everything you're doing;
You can always escape,
Race your soul to the future;
Your moments you shape
Your present you nurture.
There comes a time
When life runs by in a hurry,
That's when you close your eyes
And fantasize of what might be.
As dawn goes down today
Dusk comes slow,
Night falls my way
The peace enveloping the entire town;
Starts proclaiming the end;
To yet another day.
This moment has come again
It has left me, tired
And thus decides my brain

The Eighth Color of a Rainbow

To fast forward.
To escape the monotone
That everyday offers,
To run from the moments,
We resent;
We use the future to escape our present.

www.ingramcontent.com/pod-product-compliance
Lightning Source LLC
Chambersburg PA
CBHW030500100426
42813CB00002B/290